A souvenir guide

Peckover House and Garden
Cambridgeshire

Mike Sutherill

🏵 **National Trust**

G000162325

The Peckovers of Wisbech

Faith and harmony

This is the story of a family – the Peckovers – who between 1793 and 1948 lived in, and for many years conducted their banking business from, the house that now bears their name. From relative obscurity in the 1770s, the Peckovers rose to become one of the wealthiest and most respected families in the port town of Wisbech.

Such a rise was remarkable, the more so given that the family were Quakers, a Nonconformist religion that set them aside from society.

Below *The Presence in the Midst* by J. Doyle Penrose, 1916. Penrose, who married into the Peckover family, depicts the Quaker ideal of worship – Friends gathered in silence, listening and waiting for the presence of Christ

They were disbarred from public office, the professions and the universities, and because of their pacifist beliefs they would not enter the military. Ironically, it was their Quaker values of honesty and industriousness that attracted customers to the banking business on which the wealth of the family would be founded.

East Anglia is renowned for its nonconformity, and the Peckovers had dissent in their blood. Family members fought for Parliament during the English Civil War and were amongst the earliest followers of the Religious Society of Friends (Quaker is a sobriquet). The society was founded in the 1650s by the religious dissenter George Fox (1624–91) for individuals who wished to live by simple Christian principles without the hierarchical structures, rules and rituals imposed by the Church of England.

Quaker morals would underpin all that the Peckover family did. Each day was a gift from God to be used industriously in prayer, labour or pursuit of knowledge. The desire to explore and understand God's world led the family to

Left The unveiling of the Thomas Clarkson Memorial on 11 November 1881. The statue and canopied spire celebrating the anti-slavery campaigner was largely paid for by the Peckover family. The eminent Victorian architect Sir George Gilbert Scott, whose brother was vicar of St Peter's church in Wisbech, provided a design for the memorial. A modified version of the design was built

Right The Landing is dominated by the Venetian window overlooking the garden. The ceiling decoration is one of the finest examples of the 18th-century's plasterer's art in the country

accumulate one of the finest privately owned book collections in England, sadly sold in a series of sales after 1919. The same curiosity motivated the assemblage of *objets d'art* and the introduction of rare specimen plants in their garden.

In pursuit of knowledge the Peckovers travelled extensively across Europe and the Holy Land, returning to the comfort of the home they knew as Bank House, with its spacious rooms, fine furnishings and servants. Here they entertained business associates, family and friends. They knew the young social reformer Octavia Hill, one of the founder members of the National Trust, whose family home, now a museum, can be seen from Peckover House.

In keeping with the canons of Quakerism, the Peckovers used their wealth to aid the underprivileged. They supported the slavery abolitionist Thomas Clarkson, a son of the town, in his quest for the emancipation of slaves. They funded learning, health and recreational institutions within and beyond the town of Wisbech.

A Georgian town house

For much of the 18th and 19th centuries Wisbech was a bustling inland port with a population of about 5,000. Foreign tongues could be heard on the vessels moored along the Nene, the tidal river that flows through the town. Ships ferried produce from the surrounding fertile fenlands to the ports of London, Hull and the Continent. On their return voyage they brought back goods of all kinds – coal from the northern ports of England and silks and spices from London.

In the early 18th century Wisbech began to grow, spreading along the north bank or brink of the River Nene. Around 1722, labourers began to clear derelict farm buildings and cottages on the North Brink in preparation for the construction of what is now Peckover House. Passers-by on

Above Wisbech from Bank House, c.1840. English School. Oil painting on panel

Right Pastel on paper of Henry Southwell (1695–1762) by John Saunders. The Southwell family owned the house for 40 years and introduced the fine Rococo plasterwork and carving

Below right The Drawing Room Rococo overmantel dates from the mid-18th century. Originating in France c.1720, the Rococo style was distinguished by its use of shell and rockwork. The name is derived from *roche*, meaning rock in Middle French

Founding a banking dynasty

In 1777 young Jonathan Peckover (1755–1833) made the 40-mile journey from his home town of Fakenham in Norfolk to begin a new life in Wisbech. The next year, he opened a grocery business on the high street. Respected for his Quaker values of diligence, industry and honesty, he later provided banking facilities for his customers and in 1793, with the Gurney family, fellow Quakers of Norwich, founded the Wisbech & Lincolnshire Bank.

Two years later Jonathan and his wife Susanna Payne (1762–1853), whom he had married in 1789, rented the Southwell's house, which they later purchased. The Peckovers also owned a modest agricultural estate adjacent to the house, and over time acquired neighbouring property in order to enlarge their garden. It was during Jonathan's time that the gardens reached their present size. Jonathan remodelled one of two wings that flanked the front elevation of the house to provide a banking hall from which, for the next 70 years, the family conducted their banking business. Subsequently their home became known as Bank House.

the south bank of the river could see the red-brick house rising out of the fields on the opposite bank. Perhaps they caught a glimpse through the river mist of the bricklayers working from their flimsy scaffolding of rope-bound timber poles. Conceivably the bricks they were laying were fired in kilns across the sea in Holland and brought as ballast to Wisbech in the holds of trading vessels.

Following completion of the house, a succession of families lived there until 1752 when it was purchased by Henry Southwell, a local dignitary. His family owned the house for the next 40 years, during which time it was a hive of activity; plasterers created an intricate Rococo ceiling within the staircase hall of the house; and carvers chiselled hardwood swags, bows and garlands to create a new chimneypiece for the Drawing Room.

Jonathan Peckover and Bank House

Jonathan and Susanna raised four of their seven children here; three, not uncommonly for the time, died in infancy. Life was comfortable; Bank House was furnished with high-quality, though not ostentatious, fabrics and furniture; a maid and valet lived in the house and a cook, groom and gardeners resided in the town.

Unlike many fellow Quakers, Jonathan was not teetotal and neither were his male heirs. When entertaining family members and business associates, he served alcohol from his well-stocked cellars. Despite this rare deviation, Quaker ways were never far away. The Dining Room, its tables adorned with fine bone china, silver cutlery and candlesticks, contained a bible and stand. The bible was read aloud at mealtimes.

The Peckovers spent their time industriously in God's honour. Jonathan filled his library, now known as the Morning Room, with numerous works to gain an understanding of the world his God had created. For entertainment the family might have read aloud Shakespeare's comic plays and poetry or Cervantes' *Don Quixote*, which also graced the Library.

Knowledge also came from physically exploring God's world: the family could take the public coach to London or they might roam the countryside in their newly acquired carriage. A gig, a small two-wheeled vehicle, was used for local trips. Their riding and carriage horses were housed in a newly built stable block.

For Jonathan, industry was also to be found in

Left This watercolour of the stables is in the Peckover Sketch Book 1889. Here the groom would have cleaned the tack, using warm water from the stove, saddle soap and oil, to maintain the suppleness of the leather, prolonging its life and preventing it cracking and splitting

the garden. When writing to his son William, he recommended that the boy 'give up part of his leisure hours to the garden' and quoted the philosopher Francis Bacon who wrote that 'gardening is the purest of human pleasures'.

The winter of 1833 was a sad time at Bank House: in December Jonathan died. A few days later his coffin was carried along North Brink to the simple Quaker Meeting House in which he had prayed for much of his life. There he was laid in the earth of the town he loved. He left behind property, a fortune and a flourishing business which in 1825 he had steered through a major banking crisis.

William Peckover

On a cold December day in 1833 William Peckover (1790–1877) stood with his mother, brother and two sisters by his father's graveside. He was 43, the owner of Bank House and a partner, along with his younger brother Algernon (1803–83), in a thriving banking business. Within months of the funeral, work began on enlarging the Banking Hall, including the construction of brick-built underground vaults, the entrances to which were secured by massive steel doors provided by Chubb.

Like his father, William used his time wisely. He acquired further books for the Library and numerous antiquities from around the world.

He was a founder member of the town's museum, now the Wisbech & Fenland Museum, to which he bequeathed his collection of ancient objects and in whose care they remain.

Again like his father, William was fond of the garden, introducing geometrically arranged flower-beds and specimen trees. Because William had no children, after his death Bank House and ultimately responsibility for the family business passed to his nephew Alexander Peckover.

Above Watercolour of the old Friends Meeting House in Wisbech

Below A 19th-century view of Peckover House with the banking pavilion on the left and before the 1870s rebuilding of the east wing to create the Library

Below left Wisbech & Lincolnshire Bank note

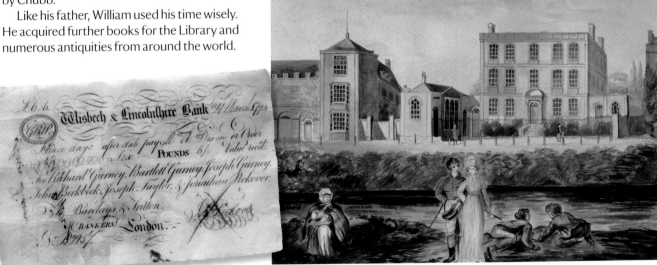

An extraordinary life

Algernon Peckover could never have envisaged what his infant son, Alexander Peckover (1830–1919), would achieve. Alexander would accomplish much that earlier generations of the family, because of their faith, could not: an honorary degree, high public office and a peerage.

Alexander was educated at Grove House, Tottenham, one of the newly founded Quaker schools. In the summer of 1848 Alexander walked the short distance from Harecroft House, his family home on North Brink, to Bank House.

Above Alexander, Baron Peckover of Wisbech by his son-in-law James Doyle Penrose, 1902. Painted in the gown of Cambridge University, which awarded him an honorary degree

Left Priscilla Hannah Peckover (1833–1931), Alexander's sister, was a talented artist and linguist and served as the president of both the Wisbech Temperance Society and Peace Association

He wrote later that he 'took up his seat on a stool and worked as an ordinary bank clerk' alongside his father, Uncle William and later his younger brother Jonathan, to learn the business.

His diary entry for 13 April 1858 recorded that 'this was the happiest day in my life…Eliza is mine'. Tragically his marriage to Eliza Sharples, daughter of a wealthy Quaker banker, was short-lived; she died in the summer of 1862, leaving a grieving Alexander to take care of their three young daughters. Alexander was fortunate in that his sister Priscilla Hannah would devote her life to bringing up her nieces. On the death of

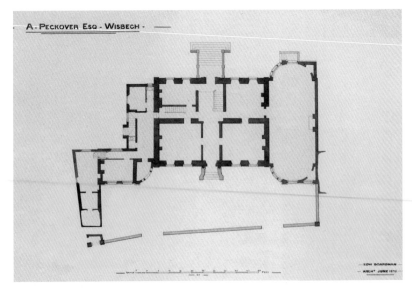

A · PECKOVER ESQ · WISBECH ·

banking premises in the town and demolition of the Banking Hall. He would be the last family member to serve the family business which merged with Barclay's and 18 other independent banks in 1896.

Alexander would achieve much in retirement: he was the first Nonconformist Lord Lieutenant of a county in Britain, though this quasi-military role was at odds with the pacifist principles of Quakerism. As a consequence he was granted a special exemption from its military duties and dress. Once denied a university education because of his faith, he was awarded an honorary degree from Cambridge University. The ultimate accolade came in 1907 when he was created Baron Peckover of Wisbech.

During the First World War, Alexander saw the dilemmas that pacifism posed for the younger generation of Quakers. He died in 1919 and was laid to rest close to his family in the Friends House graveyard.

his uncle William, Alexander, Aunt Priscilla and the girls moved into Bank House.

This quintet travelled extensively around Britain, Europe and the Holy Land, during which they recorded their journeys in a series of charming watercolours. Antiquities were collected for display and study. The family's travels to Europe's mountains prompted the creation within their garden of rockeries planted with alpines and ferns. At home Alexander used his immense wealth to support the poor and educational institutions in Wisbech and beyond.

Like his forebears, Alexander added greatly to the book collection for which a new library was built on the east side of the house in 1878. The old library became a morning room. Alexander also installed bathrooms and toilets to replace numerous portable baths and commodes in the bedrooms.

In 1893 Alexander retired aged 63, and in the winter his father died leaving Alexander a legacy with the purchasing power today of about £50 million. During Alexander's tenure the Wisbech & Lincolnshire Bank had flourished. He steered the business though a major banking crisis in 1866, and in 1877 oversaw the building of new

Above Plan dated 1879 showing the removal of the Banking Pavilion and the new Library on the right

Below The welcome parade and triumphal arch on 16 July 1907 when the newly elevated Baron Peckover returned to Wisbech

The three sisters

Alexander's daughters shared their father's values, though each developed their own distinct character and interests. The eldest, Elizabeth Josephine (1859–1930), moved to London with her artist husband James Penrose. Their son Roland, friend and biographer of Picasso, became a leading English surrealist artist. Alexandrina (1860–1948) and Anna Jane (1861–1928) remained at Bank House. Anna was said to be very shy and retiring so it came as a surprise to all when she joined the quasi-military Salvation Army. From then on the family called her 'the General'.

Alexandrina was far from shy and extremely active; she swam, skated, played tennis, rode and was a proficient mountaineer. She championed

Above The three sisters: Anna Jane, Elizabeth Josephine and Alexandrina by Elizabeth's husband, James Doyle Penrose, in about 1890

Above right Badminton on the lawn

sport in education and supported the creation of playing fields on the Peckover estate. Her intellectual pursuits were broad and she shared an interest in architecture with her grandfather Algernon. She became the first president of the Wisbech Society, established in 1939 to safeguard the historic buildings of Wisbech. Her life was not, though, without trouble: she was distressed at the sales, following her father's death in 1919, of the family book collection. More disturbing was her own perceived lack of commitment to her faith – her diary is littered with references to her spiritual struggle.

I thought my mind was more fixed on the contemplation of my God during the former part of our morning meeting but towards the end many wandering thoughts disturbed my mind; before I am aware of it I find I am thinking of worldly, vain things! Oh for strength to oppose the enemy of all good.

Alexandrina Peckover

Left Alexandrina in court dress for presentation at Buckingham Palace on 16 May 1902

Above Wedding group at the marriage of Elizabeth Josephine Peckover to the artist James Doyle Penrose in 1896

Below Alexandrina in later life

Following the loss of her dear sister Anna, Alexandrina engaged a companion to reside with her at Bank House. During the Second World War the house once more resounded with the shouts of children, evacuees from Britain's war-torn cities. They were astonished when they first saw the Dining Room, illuminated by candlelight, the table set with silver cutlery and fine china. They were captivated by the diminutive Alexandrina, dressed for dinner and adorned with a string of fine pearls.

In later life Alexandrina was often seen in the town peering through the windows of her Bentley car, which had long since replaced the family carriage. In 1943 in an act of great generosity she bequeathed Bank House (though not its contents), the garden and agricultural estate to the National Trust, at the suggestion of her nephew Alec Penrose. She continued to live there until her death in 1948. Crowds lined North Brink to see her funeral cortège travel the short distance from her home to the Friends House where she was reunited with her father, mother and sisters. Subsequently, in honour of the family with which the house had so long been associated, it was renamed Peckover House by the National Trust.

The House

Wrought in brick and stone

When c.1722 the bricklayers, carpenters, joiners and plasterers walked for the last time from the house they had built, they could be rightly proud of their labours. Few passers-by could have failed to be impressed by the house, rising three storeys against the wide East Anglian skies. The above-ground rooms provided spacious accommodation for the residents of the house while its basement accommodated the kitchen, cellars and pantries. Single-storey wings flanking the house contained a laundry and stables. Later, both wings were extensively remodelled and partially demolished.

The new house on North Brink would not have appeared out of place were it sited on one of London's fashionable streets. Its designer, probably a bricklayer or joiner, is likely to have followed guidance from one of the many architectural pattern books produced at this time. These books provided builders with detailed information ranging from the size of floor joists required to span a given opening to the size of rooms required to accommodate different functions.

Within a temporary workshop on the site, banker masons dressed the honey-coloured stone surrounds of the front and rear entrance doors and the steps of the house. Fixer masons then set the stones in place. The entrance steps at the rear of the house take advantage of the fact that the ground level at the rear is much lower than that at the front, allowing a rather gloomy dairy, accessed from the basement, to be created below the steps.

During the mid-18th century, changes were made to the rear elevation of the house with the addition of a Diocletian and a Venetian window. Such features had become fashionable in the early 18th century in very grand houses; it took time for the fashion to spread. The insertion of the windows, which enliven the rear elevation of the house, probably coincided with changes made to the staircase within the hall of the house in the mid-18th century.

Changing rooms

During the 150-year period the Peckover family lived at Bank House, successive members of the family introduced new furniture and fabric. Sadly on an autumn day in 1948, the house was the venue for a three-day sale of its contents. Almost 1,000 items went under the hammer. Fine china, paintings, mahogany furniture, silver cutlery and a stuffed cat all found new owners. Subsequently the ground-floor and basement service rooms were furnished by the National Trust. Today they appear much as they might have at the time of Alexandrina Peckover's death in 1948. One of the first-floor bedrooms has been furnished, and a museum created in another.

Above An 18th-century view of Bank House showing the original wings

Opposite The south, entrance front; a slate roof is concealed by the parapet

Below Magnified view of a sliver of paint taken from the plaster surfaces of the Banking Hall. The section shows over 15 successive paint layers. The red layer, which dates from the 1870s, was the last decorative scheme within the banking pavilion before closure

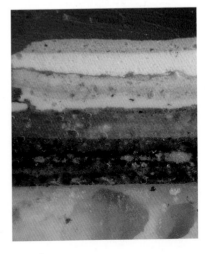

The Ground Floor

The Staircase Hall

Visitors pass, as they have for centuries, below the stone pediment marking the entrance to the house and enter its paved Hall. Alexandrina Peckover's walking stick, with its integral basket, stands ready at the rear door for her to take on a tour of the garden and collect weeds or produce. High above the staircase, lit by its large Venetian window, the ceiling is garnished with shells, garlands and flowers. Looking at the individual

Right The 'Snob Screen' above the Drawing Room window seat. Thought to date from the early 19th century, the screen provided privacy from the comings and goings to the bank

Below The Staircase Hall looking towards the front door and the river

elements of the ceiling today, its complexity is apparent, but what of the process that brought about its creation? Repeated plaster motifs such as a leaf or shell were individually cast in wooden moulds and each then attached to the ceiling. The plasterers laboured for hours, lying on scaffolding boards hand-fashioning features such as swags and garlands. Branches or metal armatures were concealed within these features to provide structural support. Finally the dry plaster would be carved with a sharp knife to provide crisp, naturalistic detail.

The Dining Room

Today four of 12 reproduction Chippendale chairs owned by the family and a late Victorian bracket clock are all that remain of their Dining Room furniture. Naturally lit by two large windows, the room is light and airy. Though electricity was introduced into the house in the 1920s, Alexandrina and Jane Peckover preferred to dine with candles casting their light on the salmon-pink walls and crimson velvet curtains. Chintz curtains that hung in this room in their great-great-grandparents' time had long gone, but the octagonal stand on which the family bible rested for over a hundred years remained.

The Drawing Room

Few can fail to be impressed by the beautifully carved Rococo overmantel mirror introduced into the Drawing Room in the 1750s. Carved in wood overlaid by a thin layer of plaster to hide the wood grain, the overmantel is of such exceptional quality that it led to a family legend, sadly untrue, that it was carved by Italian craftsmen working at Houghton Hall, Norfolk, a grand Palladian mansion built for Sir Robert Walpole, this country's first Prime Minister, in the 1720s. Whoever the craftsmen were, their skill is evident.

The room retains a pair of mid-18th-century window seats and two footstools with beadwork covers probably worked by a member of the family. When Jonathan and Susanna Peckover entertained here in the early 19th century, the walls were of a pale lilac hue while chintz fabrics covered the sofa and chairs. The pale blue dates from the second half of the 19th century.

Above left **The Dining Room.** Mirrors were placed within dining rooms in order to reflect light from the candles on the table. Typically the light from the candles would have been equivalent to the light emitted by a 30 watt electric bulb

Above right **The Drawing Room**, with a lacquer cabinet-on-stand to the right of the chimneypiece; a similar cabinet stood here until 1948

Right Elizabeth Josephine Penrose seated beside the Drawing Room fire, painted by her husband, James Penrose. She sits in one of the pair of moveable 18th-century window seats that remain in the room

The Morning Room

The Morning Room, created in the late 1870s within what was the library, is home to a cabinet of curiosities, perhaps the most important family item to remain in the house. The cabinet displays both manufactured and natural treasures: mummies, a rhino horn, minerals, watches and even bottles of water from the River Jordan. All were meticulously dusted and guarded by Alexander Peckover whose commanding voice boomed out to the children, 'Keep off dirty paws!'

Here in the Morning Room the women of the family would receive female callers, who were rarely accompanied by men. Strict rules governed the etiquette of what was a very formal ceremony. Calls were to last between 10 and 20 minutes and never exceed half an hour. The visitor's bonnet or wrap was not removed during the call.

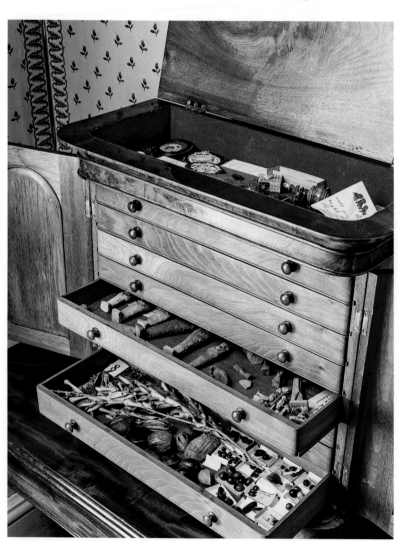

Above and left The Cabinet of Curiosities contains some 300 items, many collected on foreign tours of the Peckover family in the 19th century. Items include Hittite seals, some 3,000 years old, locks of hair and a hair brooch, Roman terracotta oil lamps and a Georgian walnut spinning top

Right The hand-blocked Cole & Son wallpaper was reproduced for the 1998–9 restoration of the Library

The Library

Completed in 1878 to designs by Edward Boardman, a notable Norwich architect, the Library was built to house Alexander Peckover's growing collection of books. Fitted book presses lined the new room which was furnished with walnut and mahogany furniture, including easy chairs, settees, card-tables, desks, a pianoforte, valuable Middle Eastern rugs and curiously a stuffed cat on a bamboo stand.

When a family member took down one of the thousands of volumes, the range of subjects they could choose from was broad: religion, architecture, natural and social history, topography and science. These works gave them access to God's world while early bibles and numerous religious texts in Greek, Latin and Hebrew, including a 10th-century gospel, brought them closer to God's word. Terrestrial and celestial globes within the Library demonstrated how God's world, the land, seas and stars, were arranged.

Sales in the early 20th century stripped the Library of its books and furniture, leaving a stark shell. Alexander's book collection was dispersed across the world. In 1998–9 the National Trust,

following Boardman's original design, reconstructed the book presses on one wall of the room. They also replicated hand-blocked wallpaper that once graced the room. The books that now furnish the library have been introduced to give some indication of the sheer quantity of works housed here in the late 19th century. Today the Wisbech & Fenland Museum owns a number of important books from the Peckover collection while the National Trust owns a handful, including Alexander's own copy of the King James Bible, a towering achievement in English literature, both beautiful and scholarly. Within the room can be seen a 12th-century copy of a 9th-century Catechesis, acquired by the National Trust in 1997. The manuscript was transcribed by Ambrosius an arthritic monk, domiciled in Greece, and used to teach the principles of Christianity.

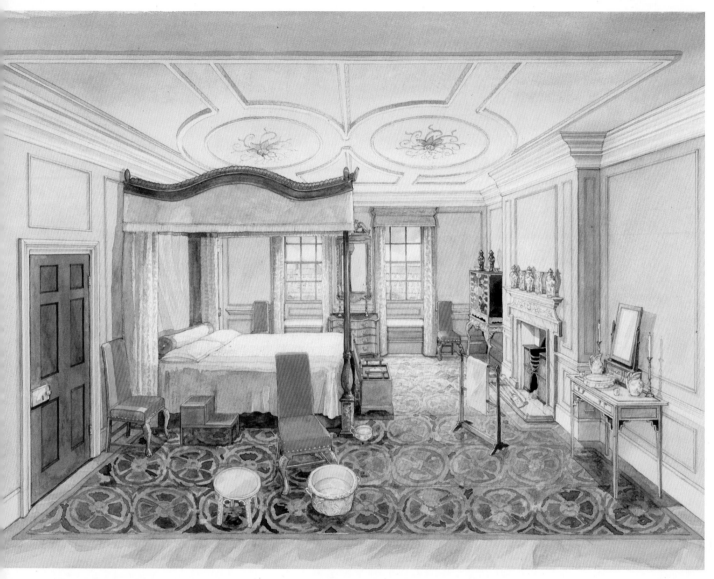

The First Floor

There were four family bedrooms on the first floor of the house and further bedrooms for family and servants on the upper floors. Today the first-floor rooms display objects outlining the history of the family, the house and town. One bedroom has been recreated as it might have appeared in the early 19th century.

Alexander, **Lord Peckover's Bedroom** is used to display temporary exhibitions. It is by far the grandest room in the house, understandable given that it once served as the main drawing room. For much of the 18th century, guests would ascend the stair to gather here to play cards, gamble or listen to music and gossip. By the early 19th century the room had been fitted

Above The Yellow Bedroom as it might have appeared in the early 19th century. A Close Stool (a portable toilet) sits at the end of the bed and a footbath stands next to the chair

up by the Peckovers as the principal bedroom, replete with a stout mahogany four-poster bed which remained in the room until its sale in 1948.

The bedroom is lit by a pair of windows, the upper shutters of which can be opened independently of the lower, allowing light to be admitted into the room while protecting the modesty of its occupants. A further aid to modesty was the provision of a door lock that could be activated via a cord by the occupant of the bed.

Lord Peckover's grandson Roland, who slept in the room adjoining his grandfather's, recalled that he was kept awake at night by Lord Peckover's recitals of Roman lyric poetry in Latin. In the morning Roland would hear the reassuring tones of Lord Peckover's butler, Cadman, announcing 'Good morning my Lord – seven twenty – damping again'. The climate of the Fens showed little variety.

The **Dressing Room** adjoining Lord Peckover's bedroom, previously an ante-room to the Drawing Room, allowed visitors to wait to be announced before entering the Drawing Room. The Dressing Room, until the building of the library in 1878, housed a number of books. Its walls were hung with paintings, sold in 1948. Today the room is graced with pictures of local interest, introduced by the National Trust.

The **Museum Room,** known in the early 19th century as the Blue Bedroom, contains objects and images relating to the family, house, Wisbech and Quakerism. Once, blue damask curtains adorned the windows and a four-poster bed stood within the room.

The **Bedroom** walls are decorated in a light stone colour, a hue used during the 18th century for the walls of almost every room within the house. The room is furnished as it might have appeared in the early 19th century. By the early 20th century the four-poster bed that once stood in the room had gone, replaced by a combination bed, which could be unfolded to create a settee or couch.

Below left Door lock

Below right *The Tribute Money,* after Sir Peter Paul Rubens (1577–1640); the overmantel in the Bedroom is probably late 18th-century

The Basement

The basement rooms of the house serviced the needs of the family. The stone-flagged **Kitchen** with its vaulted arch has changed little since it was built in the 1720s. Perhaps the greatest improvement was the introduction in the 1930s of an enamelled cast-iron stove; unlike its predecessor, which was also of cast-iron construction, the new stove did not require constant blacking and it had a temperature

Above An enamelled stove, supplied by F. Ford of Wisbech, was introduced c.1930. A small room behind the fireplace still has its 18th-century bread ovens. The Kitchen retains its stone-flagged floor

gauge. The earlier range had no such device, so assessing the heat of its ovens required skill. Parchment paper was inserted into the oven and left for a few minutes. With experience, the cook could assess the temperature by the degree to which the paper discoloured through scorching.

Before electric light was introduced in the kitchen in the 20th century, the cook worked at night by the light of the fire, the remaining daylight and the flicker of five candles in heavy iron candlesticks.

Cleverly concealed below the outdoor steps that lead down to the garden is the partly subterranean **Dairy,** kept cool by the surrounding earth. On its stone shelves were milk panakins (a small pan or metal cup), butter scales, mahogany butter trays or moulds, ham and tongue pots and milk pails. The pails were

used to bring fresh milk to the dairy from the 'milch cow' kept on the estate by the Peckovers.

The **Butler's Pantry** also remains little changed. Here the butler would have cleaned the household silver and decanted wine. Regrettably the shelves of the pantry cupboards no longer contain the family's Crown Derby tea service, hand-painted blue and gilt floral-pattern dessert service or the numerous serving dishes, silver candelabras and cutlery.

The butler was also responsible for stocking and managing the **Beer and Wine Cellars**; the former is now the gentlemen's lavatory. On Jonathan's death, his cellars held nearly 852 litres (1,500 pints) of beer held in over 20 casks and nearly 2,000 bottles containing sherry and port wine, claret, Jamaica rum, brandy and Holland gin. On Alexander Peckover's death in 1919, it is said that his daughters, who were teetotal, had the contents of the well-stocked cellars poured upon the roots of vines in the glasshouses, much to the horror of his grandsons.

At meal times the staff of Bank House gathered in the **Servants' Hall;** though not heated, it borrowed warmed air from the adjoining kitchen. From the Servants' Hall a corridor provided staff access to a back stair, avoiding the need to use the main staircase.

For much of its history the house was served by a well-equipped laundry located in the now-demolished east wing. Here the family's clothes, some 21 tablecloths, 12 kitchen-table cloths, 34 napkins and numerous sheets and towels were washed and ironed. Ironing the large cloths for the dining-table was a particularly difficult, skilled and often loathed task.

Above The outside lavatory for servants; the construction gave rise to the vulgar term 'thunderbox'

Above left The Butler's Pantry appears much as it did when Alexandrina Peckover lived in the house. The circular contraption on the counter is a rotary knife-sharpener

The Banking Hall

Though the Banking Hall was partially demolished in the 1870s, sufficient remains above ground to appreciate its former scale and layout. The surviving sections now contain the shop and an exhibition space relating the history of the Peckovers' banking business. Below ground the brick vaults that once held gold and silver coinage and the massive doors to the vaults survive little changed.

When the Wisbech & Lincolnshire Bank first opened its doors, customers entering the Banking Hall would have found themselves in a large airy room. Ranged in front of them were the clerks, equipped with scales to check the weight of coins to be deposited. A gold coin was literally worth its weight. Behind the scenes the ledgers recording the bank's financial transactions were stored on wooden shelving supported on iron brackets, sections of which survive in the exhibition space.

Banknotes first appeared in this country in the 16th century, though they had been in use in China since at least the 7th century. The Wisbech & Lincolnshire was one of many country banks, in addition to the Bank of England, to issue their own banknotes. They enabled customers to undertake financial transactions without the need to carry around valuable and heavy coins. However, as a private bank they were legally required to accept the notes they issued in exchange for gold or silver coin on demand. It was necessary therefore for the bank to have available sufficient coinage to honour the value of the notes it issued.

Early banknotes differed greatly from today's. The cashiers were required to fill in the name of the person

Left Painted and gilded tinplate hood from one of two gas lanterns formerly fixed to the front railings of the house. The lighting illuminated the front of the house and importantly improved the security of the Banking Pavilion

to be issued with the note, the date, issue number and its exact value in pounds, shillings and pence. It was then signed by the chief cashier and issued to the customer. By the time the Wisbech & Lincolnshire began issuing banknotes in the 1790s, things had changed. Banknotes were printed with fixed denominations between £20 and £1,000, the latter equivalent in purchasing value today to about £63,000. Later the process was simplified again. Instead of filling in the name of the payee and signing each note individually, the notes were printed with 'I promise to pay

Left This 19th-century blunderbuss, which despite the Peckover family's abhorrence of violence, armed the bank night-watchman. The name blunderbuss is a corruption of the Dutch term 'donderbus', from 'donder' (thunder) and 'bus' (gun)

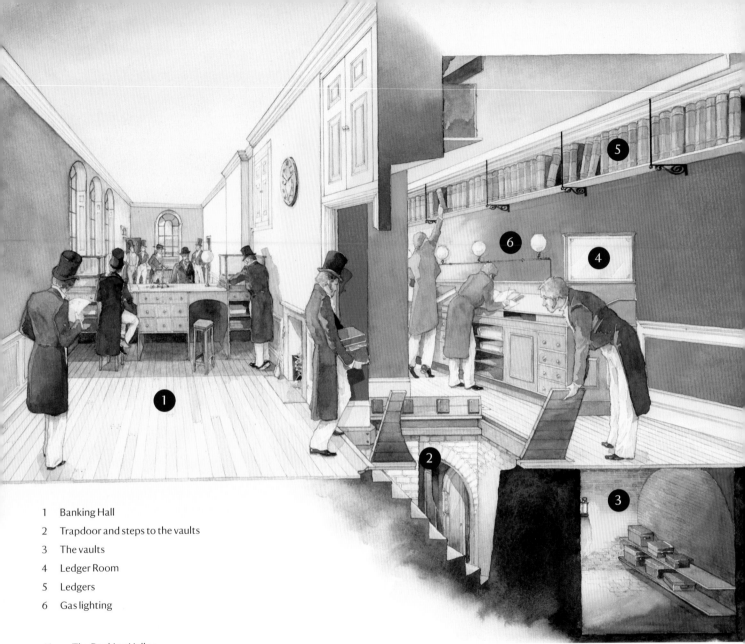

1. Banking Hall
2. Trapdoor and steps to the vaults
3. The vaults
4. Ledger Room
5. Ledgers
6. Gas lighting

Above The Banking Hall as it looked in the 1830s. The massive iron door to the vaults required activation of a release on the ground floor as well as a key in the lock, to ensure that no single person could open it the bearer on demand the sum of …', which still appears on notes today.

An Act of Parliament in 1844 gave exclusive note-issuing powers to the Bank of England; banks founded after the Act could not issue banknotes, and existing issuing banks lost their right to issue notes if and when taken over or merged. The last private bank notes in England and Wales were issued by the Somerset bank of Fox, Fowler & Co. in 1921.

The Garden and Estate

Labour and love

In the 1720s, brick walls some three metres high were constructed to the rear of the new house to enclose its soon-to-be-created garden. In keeping with the fashion of the day, the garden would be formally arranged and probably comprised a central rectangular lawn encompassed by gravel paths, edged by flower borders or pots. As with the design of the house, there was no shortage of published sources which could be consulted to determine both the layout and planting of the new garden. Nor was there a shortage of interesting plants as numerous newly discovered species began to find their way to these islands from all four corners of the world.

Above The Palm Lawn surrounded by mature trees and shrubs. The numerous pathways entice you to explore the garden further

Right Alexandrina and Anna Jane with cats on their laps

Opposite View over *Alstroemeria aurea* to a rose arch, just one of many roses which adorn the arches, pillars and walls

When the Peckovers moved into the house in the 1790s, the garden consisted only of the area immediately to the rear of the house, now known as the Palm Lawn and Wilderness Garden. Beyond this, the family owned an orchard, known today as the Productive Garden, and an adjoining yard replete with 17th-century barn (the present tea-room). Beyond the garden the family possessed a small agricultural estate.

The Productive Garden, which was planted with fruit trees, was separated from the Wilderness and Palm Lawn by neighbour William Rayner's garden. The estate, which is divided from the garden by a road, once provided a bucolic prospect when viewed from the first-floor windows of the house, its individual fields grazed by cattle or sheep, or lush with golden corn. Today the fields host sports clubs..

In 1832 the family acquired Rayner's plot, uniting the Productive Garden with the Wilderness and Palm Lawn Garden. The high walls that once separated the two gardens were retained, and a decorative garden was established

Over the next 150 years the Peckovers shaped and managed this small but beautiful area of north Cambridgeshire. Working in the garden alongside their staff was a productive use of God-given hours as well as a pleasurable pastime. It was a place of learning and joy to be shared with family and non-family members alike. The garden was often open to visitors.

The science of cultivation was important in understanding God's world. Numerous rare foreign plants were introduced into the garden. Such plants demonstrated the diversity of God's creation and satisfied the family's appetite for curiosities. Perhaps the family attitude to their garden is best summed up by the words of a fellow Quaker who wrote 'the produce of the earth is a gift from our gracious creator… to impoverish the earth to support outward greatness appears to be an injury to the succeeding age', a statement that has perhaps even more resonance today.

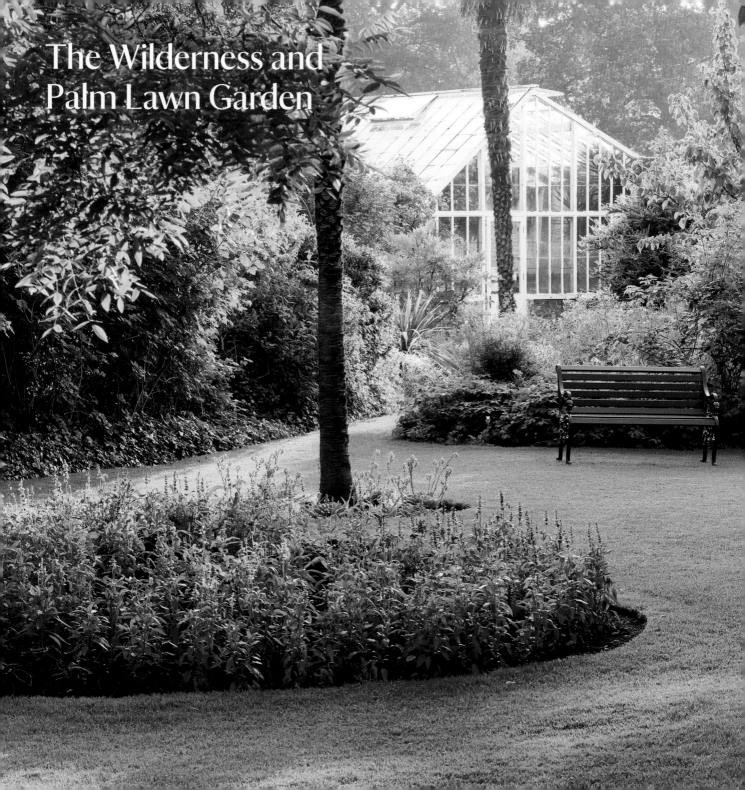

The Wilderness and Palm Lawn Garden

It seems likely that, when the Peckovers moved into the house in the 1790s, the present Wilderness and Palm Lawn Garden were at this time of formal design. In keeping with the taste of the later 18th and early 19th centuries and a desire to live in harmony with nature, the Peckovers planted woodland and specimen trees and shrubs alongside meandering paths. These specimens included a maidenhair tree, a species older than the dinosaurs, and a tulip tree, both of which can still be seen within the garden.

A glasshouse and Rustic Summer-house were built within the formal garden. It was probably Jonathan Peckover who ordered the felling of trees to provide four stout, bark-encrusted columns to support the roof of the summer-house, since rebuilt.

When William Peckover inherited the house and garden in 1833, he kept the informal layout and planting of the Wilderness and Palm Lawn. Later he introduced geometrically arranged flower-beds and a pool, both of which have been reinstated. The flower-beds were planted with annuals and roses that brought

distinct colour to the garden. William introduced a rare Chinese Chusan Palm, one of the first to be planted in this country.

By the early 20th century the glasshouse in the formal garden was in a state of dilapidation; the expertise required to tend its fruit was absent during the First World War, and fresh fruit was being replaced by cheap canned imports. Consequently half of the glasshouse was demolished and a rockery created in its place. Despite this, the garden has changed little over the years, though in the 1950s the National Trust simplified its management by removing the flower-beds and pool introduced by William. Some beds were recreated in 1999.

Today the flower borders remain planted with annuals and roses typical of those found in a Victorian garden. Many of the trees and shrubs planted by the family in the late 18th and early 19th centuries survive today, though disease has taken its toll. Species that have not thrived have been removed.

The garden united

When the family acquired William Rayner's garden in 1832 it provided a vital link between the Wilderness Garden and the Orchard. In the glasshouse now referred to as the **Orangery**, grapes were grown for the dining-table. Subsequently the vines were replaced with three Chinese orange trees, purchased from nearby Hagbeach Hall. The trees are said to have already been 200 years old when planted by the Peckovers.

Within the newly acquired garden plot, the family built a **Stable Block**, later adding a tack room. This replaced the stables housed in the west wing which were demolished around the same time to make way for the Banking Hall. The new stables, with their four elegant stalls,

Far right The Victorian Summer-house

Right The Orangery. Three very old orange trees are surrounded by a colourful seasonal display of plants in terracotta pots

Below The Stable Block is a rare example of an urban stable with its fittings intact. A horse's nameplate can be seen in the top left corner

accommodated both carriage and riding horses. The tack room was fitted out to enable the cleaning and effective storage of the carriage-horse harnesses and the bridles and saddles of the riding horses.

During the 19th century a white-painted **Summer-house** was built, and a rockery planted with ferns and alpines was created. The Summer-house, glasshouse and paths within this part of the garden would still be familiar to Alexandrina, though the rockery no longer survives. The current planting within the garden was largely designed by Graham Stuart Thomas, garden advisor to the National Trust from 1955 to 1975.

The Orchard Garden

For many years the Orchard Garden provided pears, apples, quince, cherries and damsons for the dining-table of Bank House. In keeping with the family's Quaker ethics, the fruit was shared with the less fortunate. In a shady spot the family buried their beloved cats. The headstones commemorate the passing of Angel, Zeta, Bijou, Marmie and Pharos, Alexander's 'much beloved and beautiful tabby cat'.

In the mid-19th century, carpenters erected a new glasshouse within the Orchard Garden. Known as a **Propagation House**, it is a type designed specifically for raising plants. The floor of the building is sunk below ground level, an arrangement thought to retain heat to encourage plant growth. The Propagation House was probably constructed in order to provide the large number of annuals for the flower

Below The Centenary Border where bulbs, perennials and dahlias provide colour for over nine months of the year

Above The Red Border. Plants with dark foliage mingle with blooms in various shades of red to create a striking vista

borders created by William in the Wilderness. The Propagation House was rebuilt in 2009 using aluminium framing and continues to provide plants for the numerous flower borders within the gardens.

Under National Trust stewardship, new flower borders have been introduced within the Orchard Garden. The Red Border is vibrant with tulips in spring, while in summer tender perennials such as dahlias, salvias and cannas are planted amidst permanent plantings of roses and herbaceous perennials. The Centenary Border, rich in pastel colours, was laid out in 1995 to celebrate the 100th anniversary of the founding of the National Trust. Not surprisingly it includes the rose 'Octavia Hill'.

The Orchard Lawn area still pays homage to the fruit-growing interests of the Peckovers; espalier pears, a damson, quince and apple trees grow in this section of the garden.

Adjoining the garden is the 17th-century **Reed Barn,** the last vestige of the farmstead demolished to make way for the house. It once witnessed the threshing of wheat harvested from the surrounding farmland. Later the barn provided additional stabling for the family's horses. During the Second World War it served as a theatre providing respite from the austerity of war for civilians and service personnel alike. Today it is the National Trust tea-room. Within the courtyard the cobbles are laid out in a pattern that reflects the layout of a privet maze that once stood within the wider estate.

The estate

Extending to 19.4 hectares (48 acres), the Peckovers' agricultural estate was made up of a patchwork of fields, each delineated by neatly laid hedgerows interspersed with woodland trees. These trees demarcated the perimeter of the Peckovers' estate and provided shelter for the livestock and crops from the fenland winds.

Today the old field patterns, hedgerows and trees broadly survive and more trees have been planted. In keeping with Alexandrina Peckover's wish to encourage sporting activities, the estate now provides a rare green space within the urban landscape of Wisbech where cricket, hockey, rugby and football flourish. Now the bleat of sheep has given way to the sound of leather on willow and the shrieks of children.

Below The south front and the gardens, with the Orangery and Propagation House at the bottom right-hand corner